I can draw
Animals

DK

LONDON, NEW YORK, MUNICH, MELBOURNE, and DELHI

DESIGNED BY Penny Lamprell
ILLUSTRATED BY Jenny Williams
& the Peter Bull Art Studio
WRITTEN AND EDITED BY Lorrie Mack
US EDITOR Margaret Parrish
PHOTOGRAPHY BY Andy Crawford
PUBLISHING MANAGER Susan Leonard
JACKET DESIGNER Karen Hood
JACKET EDITOR Carrie Love
PRODUCTION Seyhan Esen-Yagmurlu
DTP DESIGNER Almudena Díaz
CONSULTANT Emma Drew

First American Edition, 2006

Published in the United States by
DK Publishing, Inc., 375 Hudson Street
New York, New York 10014

06 07 08 09 10 10 9 8 7 6 5 4 3 2 1

Copyright © 2006 Dorling Kindersley
Limited

All rights reserved. No part of this
publication may be reproduced, stored in a
retrieval system, or transmitted in any form
or by any means, electronic, mechanical,
photocopying, recording, or otherwise,
without the prior written permission of the
copyright owner. Published in Great Britain
by Dorling Kindersley Limited.

A Cataloging-in-Publication record
for this book is available from the
Library of Congress.

ISBN-13 978-0-7566-1987-9
ISBN-10 0-7566-1987-4

Color reproduction by ICON,
United Kingdom
Printed and bound in Slovakia
by Tlaciarne BB S.R.O.

Discover more at
www.dk.com

Contents

I'm hopping to see you on page 12

See me up close on page 8

Woof! Woof! Learn how to draw me on page 14

Look for my mom and me on page 24

Find me on page 18

My friends are flying on page 42

Useful stuff

COLLECT LOTS OF DIFFERENT artists' materials so your drawings can be as varied as possible. When you have time, experiment with all your pens and pencils to discover new effects you can create.

charcoal stick

use an eraser or a finger to smudge charcoal like this

eraser

soft pencil, for shading

No. 2 pencil
for outline

sketch pad

pencil
sharpener

colored
paper

colored pencils

soft pastels
are powdery and smudgeable—good for soft shadows and blending

oil pastels are greasy and a bit hard to blend—use them for rough textures like elephant skin

Something to follow

From magazines, cut out pictures of all the animals you want to draw and keep them for reference. Stuffed animals can show you how your creatures look in 3-D, and odd feathers will help you to get your bird wings and tails just right.

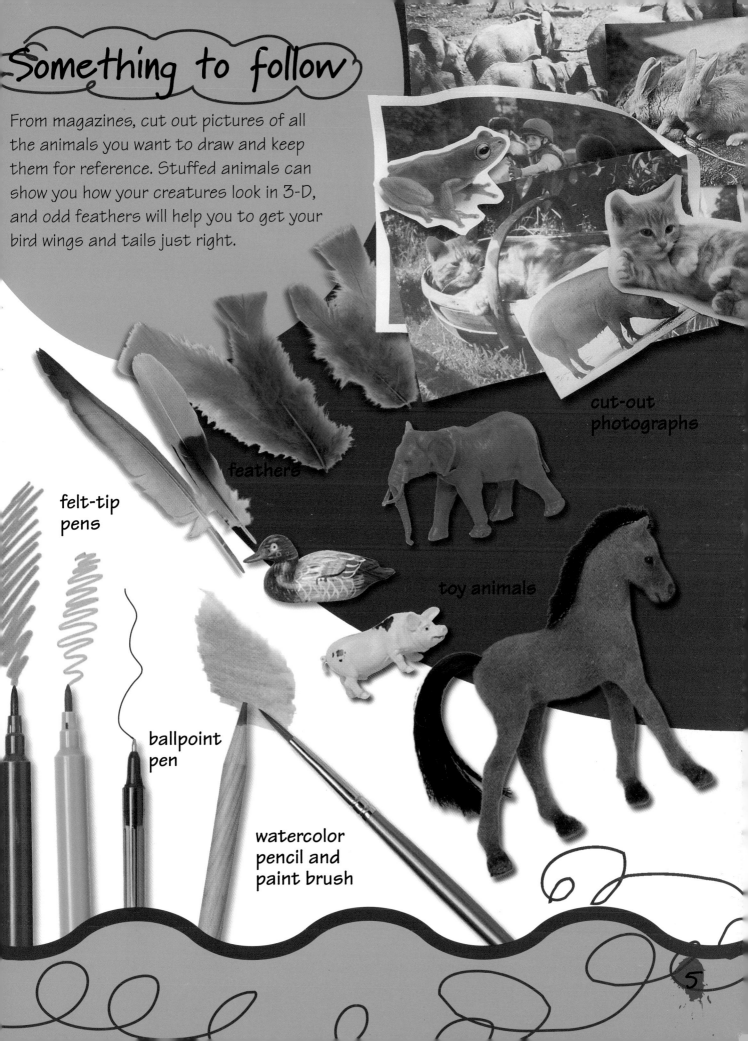

cut-out
photographs

feathers

felt-tip
pens

toy animals

ballpoint
pen

watercolor
pencil and
paint brush

Animal gallery

FOLLOW OUR STEP-BY-STEP instructions for drawing lots of animals like the ones shown here. Start with a fluffy chick and you'll soon be working on a huge jungle elephant!

Owl

Pony

Piglet

Frog

Puppies

Bear cubs

Elephant

Duckling

Duckling

Lamb

Mouse

Kittens

Hen and chicks

7

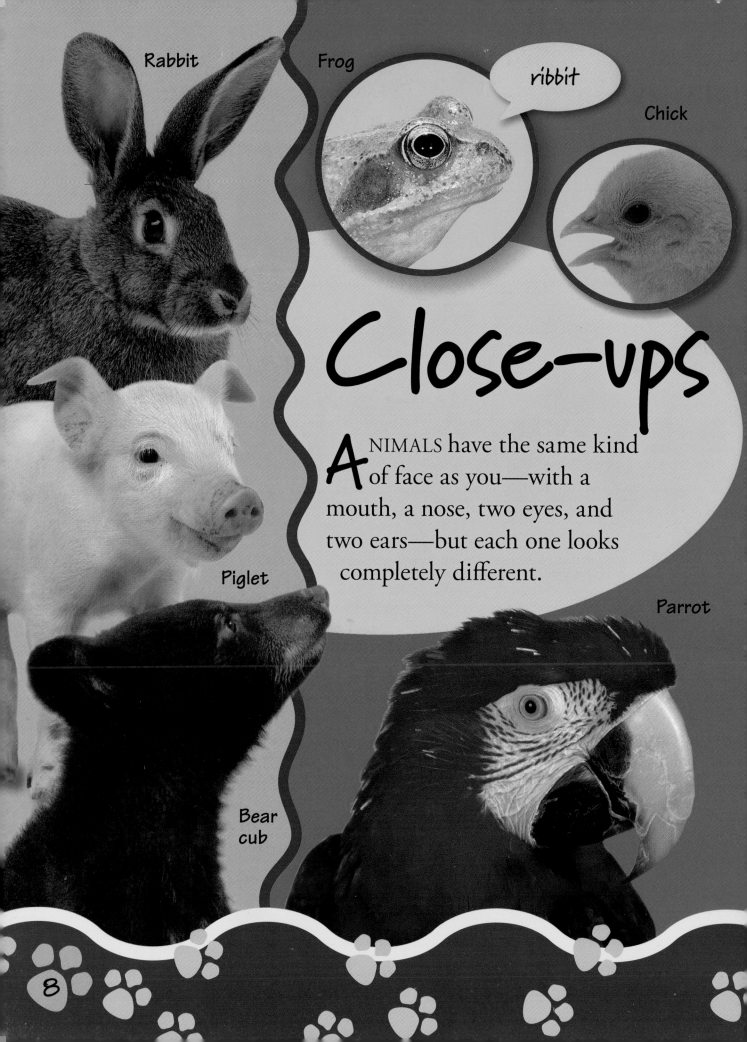

Rabbit

Frog

ribbit

Chick

Close-ups

ANIMALS have the same kind of face as you—with a mouth, a nose, two eyes, and two ears—but each one looks completely different.

Piglet

Parrot

Bear
cub

Arrange big circles and small ones to make a basic shape.

Link all the circles with curved lines to form your outline.

Kitten

KITTENS LOVE TO PLAY. They have sharp claws that tangle yarn and long, curly tails they can chase. To keep their fur clean, they lick their paws and rub it.

Draw the ears and fill in her mouth, nose, and eyes.

Add finishing touches like whiskers and shaded fur.

Use lines of shading on the kitten's body to suggest her warm, soft coat.

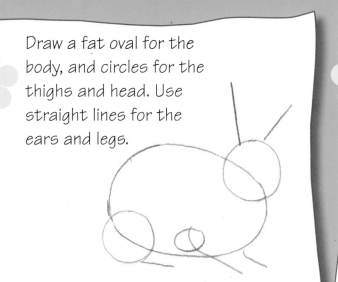

1 Draw a fat oval for the body, and circles for the thighs and head. Use straight lines for the ears and legs.

2 Make an outline that links and rounds out all the shapes you have drawn.

Rabbit

RABBITS HAVE LONG, FLOPPY ears and a short fluffy tail. Their favorite foods are green, leafy plants that grow in farmers' fields and people's backyards.

3 Fill in details on the ears, the paws, and the face—and add whiskers!

Use shading to make your bunny's fur look silky, soft, and warm.

1

As well as circles, you'll need ovals and a rectangle to start your drawing off.

2

Join the shapes to form an outline, rounding out the legs at the same time.

3

Now give your puppy toes, long ears, and a black nose that can smell trouble.

Puppy

WITH HIS FLOPPY EARS and big eyes, this puppy looks very innocent, but don't be fooled—he's looking for mischief!

woof! woof!

Your puppy could have a fluffy, hairy coat or a smooth one with lots of spots.

Odds and ends

WE CAN SPOT A FEW ANIMALS by one unique part of their body: an elephant's trunk, for example, or a pig's snout. But creatures that are very different sometimes have similar features—like kittens' and puppies' paws, or the wings on a parrot and an owl.

Puppy

Ear, ear

Rabbit

Kitten

Piglet

Wonderful wings

Owl

Parrot

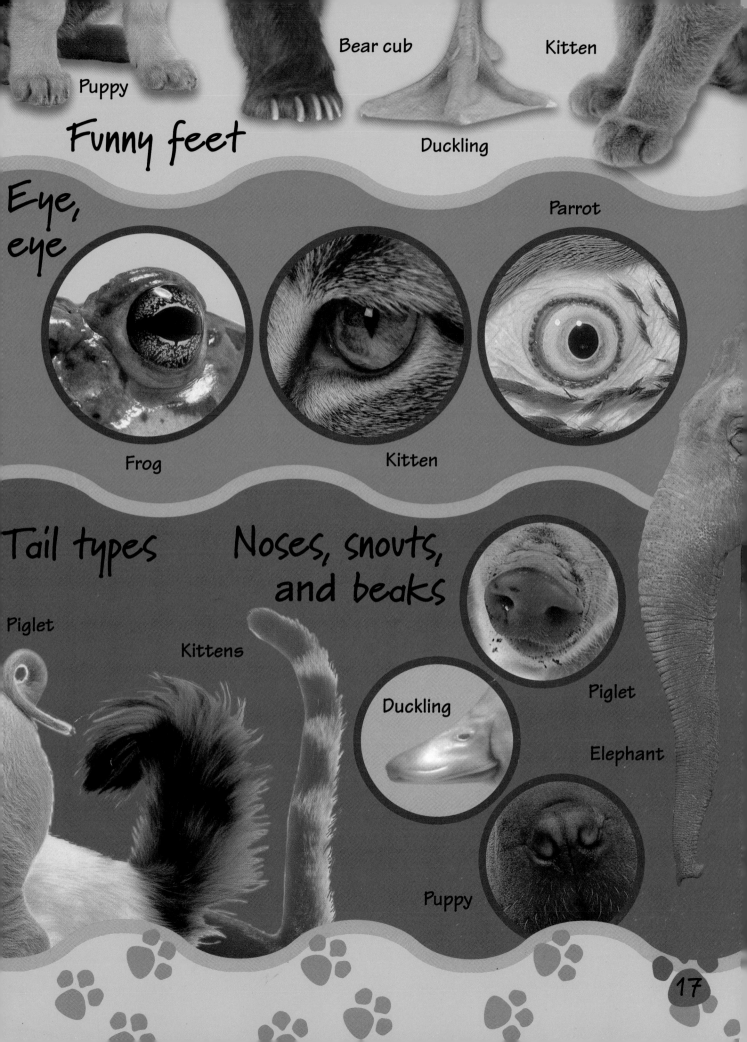

Puppy

Bear cub

Kitten

Funny feet

Duckling

Eye, eye

Parrot

Frog

Kitten

Tail types

Noses, snouts, and beaks

Piglet

Kittens

Duckling

Piglet

Elephant

Puppy

Chick

BABY CHICKS PECK their way out of their mother's eggs. The tiny newborns are yellow with soft, fluffy feathers.

1 Overlap circles to make rough shapes for the head and body.

cheep! cheep!

Fill in the textures on his feet and feathers.

2 Add a few linking curves to form your outline.

3 Draw details of his face, wings, and tail.

1 Start with sausage shapes, then add lines for the neck and tail, and lines and circles for the legs.

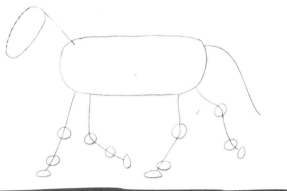

2 Draw an outline of the pony's body by linking the shapes.

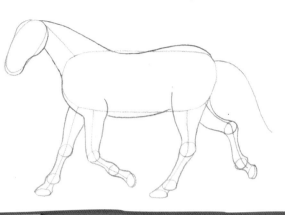

Pony

DRAW YOUR VERY own pony so you can dream about grooming him and taking him out for long rides.

3 Fill in the tail, the mane, the forelock, and the ears.

4 Add details on his face and hooves, and texture on his mane and tail.

Shading makes his face and dappled coat more lifelike.

1

Make the basic shape with one big oval and circle, eight little circles, and a few lines.

2

Connect them to make an outline, adding hooves, ears, and chubby legs as you go.

3

Now draw his loopy tail, piggy eyes, and big snout, and add a bit of shading on his ears.

Soft shading makes his legs and body look round and realistic.

Piglet

oink !
oink !

LIKE GROWN-UP PIGS, babies use their wide, flat snouts to sniff for food in the ground. They keep bugs off their skin by rolling around in the mud.

1 Start with circles, sausage shapes, and a few lines.

2 Join your shapes to make the outline, then add mouth, ears, and hooves.

Lamb

L ITTLE LAMBS live in big groups called herds with their families and friends. When they grow up, their thick coats will be cut off and made into wool.

3 Put details on his face, suggest wool with squiggles, and add some grass.

baa baa!

Use lots of tiny curls and circles for texture.

No. 2 pencil, *for general outline*

soft pencil, *for shading*

colored pencil, *for soft color*

felt-tip pen, *for strong color*

Shading

USE DIFFERENT KINDS of shading to make your animals look more exciting and real.

Try out different pens and pencils to get the effects you want.

ribbit, ribbit!

pastel, *for soft color*

charcoal stick, *for soft edges*

eraser, *for smudging*

26

Types of shading

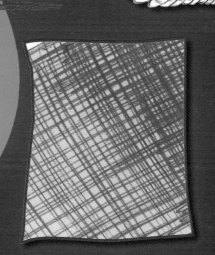

Diagonal lines will add depth to your drawing. For darker shading, make them closer together.

For crosshatching, make lots of straight lines, then add more lines going the other way.

Stippling is using lots of tiny dots to create different levels of shading.

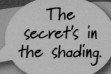

The secret's in the shading.

Details that count

See how flat and dull the piglet above looks compared to the tubby, lifelike one on the right. What a difference some shade makes!

27

1 Start with a small teardrop shape and a large one, then add circles and lines for his legs, tail, and ears.

2 Draw your outline. Fill in his legs and feet, his smooth tube-shaped tail, and his ears, mouth, and nose.

3 Add eyes, long whiskers, and a bit of fur around the edges.

Mouse

Squeak, squeak!

IS THERE A MOUSE in your house? Maybe—house mice live all over the world, except in the Arctic and the Antarctic.

Use your shading skills to make his fur coat look thick and soft.

29

1. Draw a sausage-shaped body that narrows at one end. Add circles and sticks for the head and legs, more circles for the ears, and curved lines for the muzzle.

2. Round out the body and legs, adding a gentle bump on your cub's back. Now use your eraser to make some of your basic shapes less obvious.

3. Fill in the detail on his face, ears, and claws, then use small jagged scribbly lines to indicate his rough fur.

Bear cub

BABY BEARS ARE BORN blind and bald, but after a few months, they can see, they have a furry coat, and they like to play together.

growl, growl!

Texture will make your cub's coat lifelike.

Frog

HAPPY TO LIVE in water or on land, frogs have long, strong back legs so they can jump very far and very high.

1 Arrange two eyelike shapes for the frog's body. Add circles for his eyes, and ovals and lines for his legs.

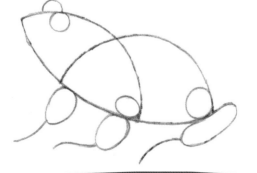

2 Link the shapes to form your outline, then round out the legs and add three webbed feet.

Shading works just as well for
showing smooth shiny skin as it
does for suggesting fur.

3　Fill in the eyes, mouth, and nose,
and draw the last webbed foot and
the small bump on his back.

4　Start giving your frog's skin some
color and texture, and add a pale
stripe down his back.

1 Start with lots of circles and a few curved lines.

2 Draw an outline around the shapes, adding a pointed tail and beak, plus legs and feet.

3 Fill in your duckling's eye, beak, and wing, and ruffle up a few of his feathers!

Duckling

DUCKS ARE VERY SMART birds—
they can fly *and* they can swim.
Even the babies have soft, oily feathers
that keep them warm and dry inside.

Use lots of short, light
strokes to fill in your
duckling's waterproof
feathers.

Texture

U SE YOUR NEW SKILLS and all your artists' materials to add depth and texture to the animals you draw.

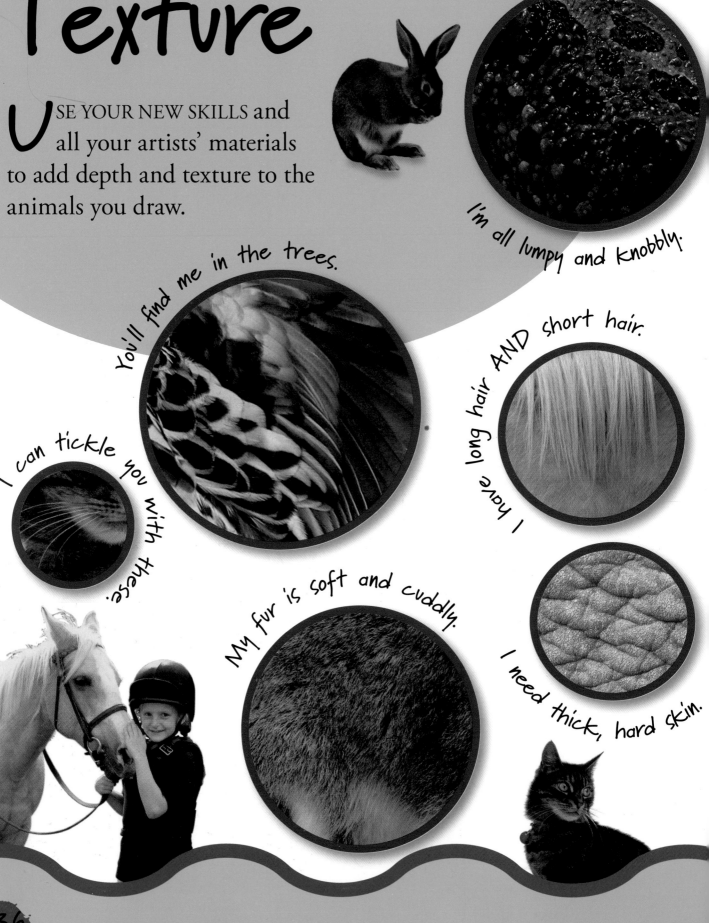

I'm all lumpy and knobbly.

You'll find me in the trees.

I can tickle you with these.

I have long hair AND short hair.

My fur is soft and cuddly.

I need thick, hard skin.

Texture tips

Show the soft fur on kittens and rabbits with light, smudged lines.

Tough pig or elephant hide needs thick, strong texture marks.

Bring feathers to life using long delicate strokes filled in with short soft ones.

Words to think about

scaly furry bumpy lumpy smooth slimy hairy prickly spiky feathery shiny

I'm very furry —I need soft edges.

1 Use circles, a cone, two sideways teardrops, and a few lines to make your basic owl shape.

2 Join the shapes to make an outline, then draw the claws and face, and a few wing and tail feathers.

3 Take time to sketch in lots of curvy, graceful feathers on your owl's wings and tail.

A little soft shading brings your owl's face, body, and wings magically to life.

Owl

TUWHIT TUWHOO! Barn owls have sweet heart-shaped faces, but they are fierce hunters who eat rats and mice.

1 Draw lots of circles, some overlapping, and curvy lines for your chipmunk's legs and tail.

2 Make an outline by linking your shapes, drawing a round tail and limbs, and adding a pointy face.

Chipmunk

WHEN THEY FIND yummy nuts and seeds to eat, chipmunks carry them home inside their pouchy cheeks.

3 Add ears, a tiny eye, and claws that look like hands and feet.

4 Now draw whiskers and use shading to suggest a stripey coat.

Use lots of short lines to provide texture that fades from dark to light. This creates the impression of fur.

Parrot

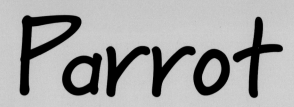

AT HOME IN STEAMY jungles, parrots are very, very noisy, with sharp bills and lots of bright feathers.

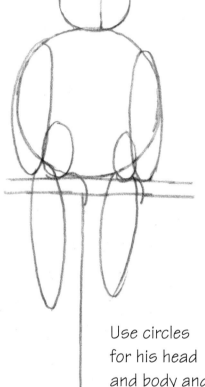

1

Use circles for his head and body and squashed ovals for his wings. Draw a perch for him to sit on.

2

Draw the basic shape of his long tail feathers and his hooked beak.

3

Add sharp claws around the perch, a beady eye, and more detailing on all his feathers.

Squawk! Squawk!

Use short, soft lines to give texture to his claws, his feathers, his beak, and his wooden perch.

43

1 Use circles and ovals for the head, body, and legs, and long lines for the trunk and tail.

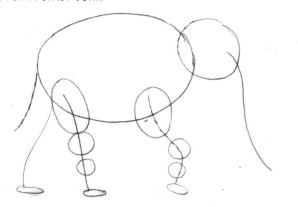

2 Shape the legs and feet, then the body, trunk, and tail.

Elephant

THIS HUGE BEAST has a long trunk to smell, eat, and drink with, and enormous ears that he uses like giant fans to cool himself down.

3 Add big floppy ears, pointed tusks, toes, and a paintbrushy tip to the tail.

4 Fill in your elephant's eye and start to add texture to his skin.

Bring his rough, thick, bumpy skin to life with subtle shading.

Scale

SOME ANIMALS, LIKE MICE, chicks, and frogs, are so tiny you could hold one in your hand. But adult elephants and ponies are MUCH bigger than you!

Sensible sizes

If you draw more than one animal on the page, try to make sure they're all roughly the right size in relation to each other. A big mouse would look silly next to a tiny bear!

Near or far

When you're drawing a whole picture, remember that the closer objects are to the front, the bigger they should be.

Woof!

Baby elephants are bigger than grown-up dogs!

Index

woof woof, bye bye!

Acknowledgments

Dorling Kindersley would like to thank: Marie Bernadette Greenwood for editorial support; Karen Hood, Tory Gordon-Harris, and Jane Bull for design inspiration; Rose Horridge for picture research; Zahavit Shalev and Fleur Star for editorial assistance.

Picture credits

Picture credits t = top b = bottom c = center l = left r = right
Picture montage on top right of page 5: Paul Bricknell © Dorling Kindersley 5br. John Daniels © Dorling Kindersley 5cr. Christopher & Sally Gable © Dorling Kindersley 5t. David Handley © Dorling Kindersley 5c. Jacqui Hurst © Dorling Kindersley 5bl. Bill Ling © Dorling Kindersley 5bc. Chris Mattison © Dorling Kindersley 5cl. Jane Miller © Dorling Kindersley 5tr. All other images © Dorling Kindersley www.dkimages.com